I0434988

U.S. Fish & Wildlife Service

Draft Comprehensive Conservation Plan and Environmental Assessment
Bear Butte National Wildlife Refuge

February 2007

Prepared by the U.S. Fish and Wildlife Service

Bear Butte National Wildlife Refuge
29746 Bird Road
Martin, SD 57551

and

Division of Refuge Planning, Region 6
134 Union Boulevard, Suite 300
Lakewood, CO 80228

Contents

List of Figures and Tables

Figures

Tables

Abbreviations

CCP	comprehensive conservation plan
CD	compatibility determination
EA	environmental assessment
EO	executive order
FONSI	finding of no significant impact
Improvement Act	National Wildlife Refuge System Improvement Act of 1997
NEPA	National Environmental Policy Act of 1969
the refuge	Bear Butte National Wildlife Refuge
Refuge System	National Wildlife Refuge System
SDGFP	South Dakota Game, Fish, and Parks Department
Service or USFWS	U.S. Fish and Wildlife Service
State	state of South Dakota

Bear Butte National Wildlife Refuge was established as a limited-interest refuge in the late 1930s with the acquisition of easements from private landowners, the state of South Dakota, and the War Department (now transferred to the Bureau of Land Management at Ft. Meade) to maintain an area for "migratory bird, wildlife conservation, and other purposes." The refuge is 374.20 easement acres and has no fee title.

The U.S. Fish and Wildlife Service entered into a cooperative agreement with the state of South Dakota on July 12, 1967, to administer, operate, and maintain the refuge pursuant to the rights and interests in real property acquired by the United States, and more particularly described in the easement agreement.

This draft comprehensive conservation plan has been prepared by a planning team composed of representatives from various U.S. Fish and Wildlife Service programs, including the refuge staff, and in consultation with the South Dakota Game, Fish, and Parks Department.

PURPOSES OF ESTABLISHMENT

The purposes of the refuge are as follows:

Executive Order, August 26, 1935 "as a refuge and breeding ground for migratory birds and other wildlife."

Migratory Bird Conservation Act "for use as an inviolate sanctuary, or for any other management purpose, for migratory birds."

THE PLANNING PROCESS

This draft comprehensive conservation plan and environmental assessment for the refuge was mandated by the National Wildlife Refuge System Improvement Act of 1997. Once an alternative is selected, it will be carried out within the 15-year life of the plan.

ALTERNATIVES

Two alternatives were evaluated during the planning process. The no-action alternative, describes the current and future management of the refuge. Under the no-action alternative, the U.S. Fish and Wildlife Service would continue to manage the refuge within the parameters of the cooperative agreement. Existing habitat within the easement and all public programs would continue to be administered and maintained by the South Dakota Game, Fish, and Parks Department.

© 2005 Laura Crawford Williams

American Avocet

The proposed action is to relinquish the easement to current landowners. Under this alterative, Bear Butte National Wildlife Refuge would be taken out of the National Wildlife Refuge System and the easements would be transferred to the current landowners. Under this alternative, the U.S. Fish and Wildlife Service's requirements would no longer exist. It would divest its interest in the refuge.

1 Introduction

The U.S. Fish and Wildlife Service (Service) has developed this draft comprehensive conservation plan (CCP) to use as a guide in analyzing whether Bear Butte National Wildlife Refuge (the refuge) meets the intent of the National Wildlife Refuge System (Refuge System) Improvement Act of 1997 (Improvement Act).

The plan was developed in compliance with the Improvement Act and part 602 (Refuge System Planning) of the Service manual. The actions described within this plan also meet the requirements of the National Environmental Policy Act of 1969 (NEPA). Compliance with this act is being achieved through the involvement of the public and the inclusion of an integrated environmental assessment (EA).

The refuge was established as a limited-interest refuge in the late 1930s with the acquisition of easements from private landowners, the state of South Dakota (State), and the War Department (now transferred to Bureau of Land Management at Ft. Meade) to maintain an area for "migratory bird, wildlife conservation, and other purposes." The refuge is 374.20 easement acres and has no fee title. The easement obtained from the State only applies to lands below the ordinary high-water mark of the lake. A cooperative agreement was entered into with the State on July 12, 1967, to administer, operate, and maintain the refuge pursuant to the rights and interest in real property acquired by the United States, and more particularly described in the easement agreements.

The plan has been prepared by a planning team composed of representatives from various Service programs, including the refuge staff, and in consultation with the South Dakota Game, Fish, and Parks Department (SDGFP).

After reviewing public comments and management needs, the planning team developed a preferred alternative. This alternative will attempt to address all significant issues while determining how best to achieve the intent and purposes of the refuge. The preferred alternative is the Service's recommended course of action for the future management of this refuge, and is embodied in this draft.

PURPOSE AND NEED FOR PLAN

The purpose of this draft CCP is to identify the role that the refuge will play in support of the mission of the Refuge System, and to provide long-term guidance to management programs and activities. The plan is needed to:

- provide a clear statement of direction for the future management of the program;
- provide landowners, neighbors, visitors, and government officials with an understanding of the Service's management actions on and around this refuge;
- ensure that the Service's management actions are consistent with the mandates of the Improvement Act of 1997, and;
- ensure that the management of this refuge is consistent with federal, state, and county plans.

Bear Butte

THE U.S. FISH AND WILDLIFE SERVICE AND THE NATIONAL WILDLIFE REFUGE SYSTEM

THE U.S. FISH AND WILDLIFE SERVICE

"The mission of the U.S. Fish and Wildlife Service, working with others, is to conserve, protect, and enhance fish and wildlife and their habitats for the continuing benefit of the American people."

Today, the Service enforces federal wildlife laws, manages migratory bird populations, restores nationally significant fisheries, conserves and restores vital wildlife habitat, protects and recovers endangered species, and helps other governments with conservation efforts. It also administers a federal aid program that distributes hundreds of millions of dollars to states for fish and wildlife restoration, boating access, hunter education, and related projects across America.

THE NATIONAL WILDLIFE REFUGE SYSTEM

In 1903 President Theodore Roosevelt designated the 5.5-acre Pelican Island in Florida as the nation's first wildlife refuge for the protection of brown pelicans and other native nesting birds. This was the first time the federal government set aside land for the sake of wildlife. This small but significant designation was the beginning of the Refuge System. One hundred years later, this system has become the largest collection of lands in the world specifically managed for wildlife, encompassing over 96 million acres within 544 refuges and over 3,000 small areas for waterfowl breeding and nesting. Today, there is at least one refuge in every state in the nation, as well as in Puerto Rico and the U.S. Virgin Islands.

In 1997 a clear mission was established for the Refuge System through the passage of the Improvement Act. That mission is:

"... to administer a national network of lands and waters for the conservation, management, and, where appropriate, restoration of the fish, wildlife, and plant resources and their habitats within the United States for the benefit of present and future generations of Americans." (Improvement Act)

The Improvement Act further states that each refuge shall:

- fulfill the mission of the Refuge System;
- fulfill the individual purposes of each refuge;
- consider the needs of fish and wildlife first;
- develop a CCP for each unit of the Refuge System, and fully involve the public in the preparation of these plans;
- maintain the biological integrity, diversity, and environmental health of the Refuge System;
- recognize that wildlife-dependent recreational activities, including hunting, fishing,

wildlife observation and photography, and environmental education and interpretation, are legitimate and priority public uses;

- retain the authority of refuge managers to determine compatible public uses.

In addition to the overall mission of the Refuge System, the wildlife and habitat vision for each refuge stresses the following principles:

- Fish and wildlife come first.
- Ecosystems, biodiversity, and wilderness are vital concepts in refuge management.
- Refuges must be healthy.
- Growth of refuges must be strategic.
- The Refuge System serves as a model for habitat management with broad participation from others.

Following passage of the Improvement Act, the Service immediately began efforts to carry out the direction of the new legislation, including the preparation of CCPs for all refuges. The development of these plans is now occurring nationally. Consistent with the Improvement Act, all refuge CCPs are being prepared in conjunction with public involvement, and each refuge is required to complete its own plan within the fifteen-year schedule (by 2012).

DECISION TO BE MADE

The Mountain-Prairie regional director of the Service will select the alternative that will be implemented as the refuge's CCP. This decision will be made in recognition of the environmental effects of each alternative considered. The decision will be disclosed in a Finding of No Significant Impact (FONSI) included in the final CCP. Implementation of the CCP will begin once the regional director has signed the FONSI.

PEOPLE AND THE NATIONAL WILDLIFE REFUGE SYSTEM

Our fish and wildlife heritage contributes to the quality of our lives and is an integral part of our Nation's greatness. People and nature are linked through spiritual, recreational, and cultural ties. Wildlife and wild places have always given people special opportunities to have fun, relax, and appreciate our natural world.

ECOSYSTEM DESCRIPTIONS AND THREATS

MISSOURI RIVER MAIN STEM

The Service has adopted watersheds as the basic building blocks for implementing ecosystem conservation. The refuge is located in the Missouri River Main Stem Ecosystem. This vast area covers all of North Dakota and South Dakota and small portions of Nebraska, Wyoming, and Montana. The major threats identified for this ecosystem include conversion of prairie to cropland, overgrazing, invasive species, and aggressive prairie dog control. The Service contributes to the accomplishment of goals for this ecosystem through its Partners for Fish and Wildlife Program.

NATIONAL AND REGIONAL MANDATES

The administration of the Refuge System is guided by a variety of international treaties, federal laws, and presidential executive orders (EOs). Management options under each refuge's establishing authority and the Improvement Act are contained in the documents and acts.

THE PLANNING PROCESS

This draft CCP and EA is intended to comply with the Improvement Act and NEPA and their implementing regulations. The Service issued a final refuge planning policy in 2000 that established requirements and guidance for Refuge

System planning, including CCPs, ensuring that planning efforts comply with the provisions of the Improvement Act. The planning policy identified several steps of the CCP and EA process (see figure 1):

- Form a planning team and conduct pre-planning.
- Initiate public involvement and scoping.
- Draft vision statement and goals and determine significant issues.
- Develop and analyze alternatives, including proposed action.
- Prepare draft CCP and EA.
- Prepare and adopt final CCP and EA and issue a FONSI (or determine whether an environmental impact statement is needed).
- Implement plan, monitor and evaluate.
- Review plan (every 5 years) and revise (every 15 years).

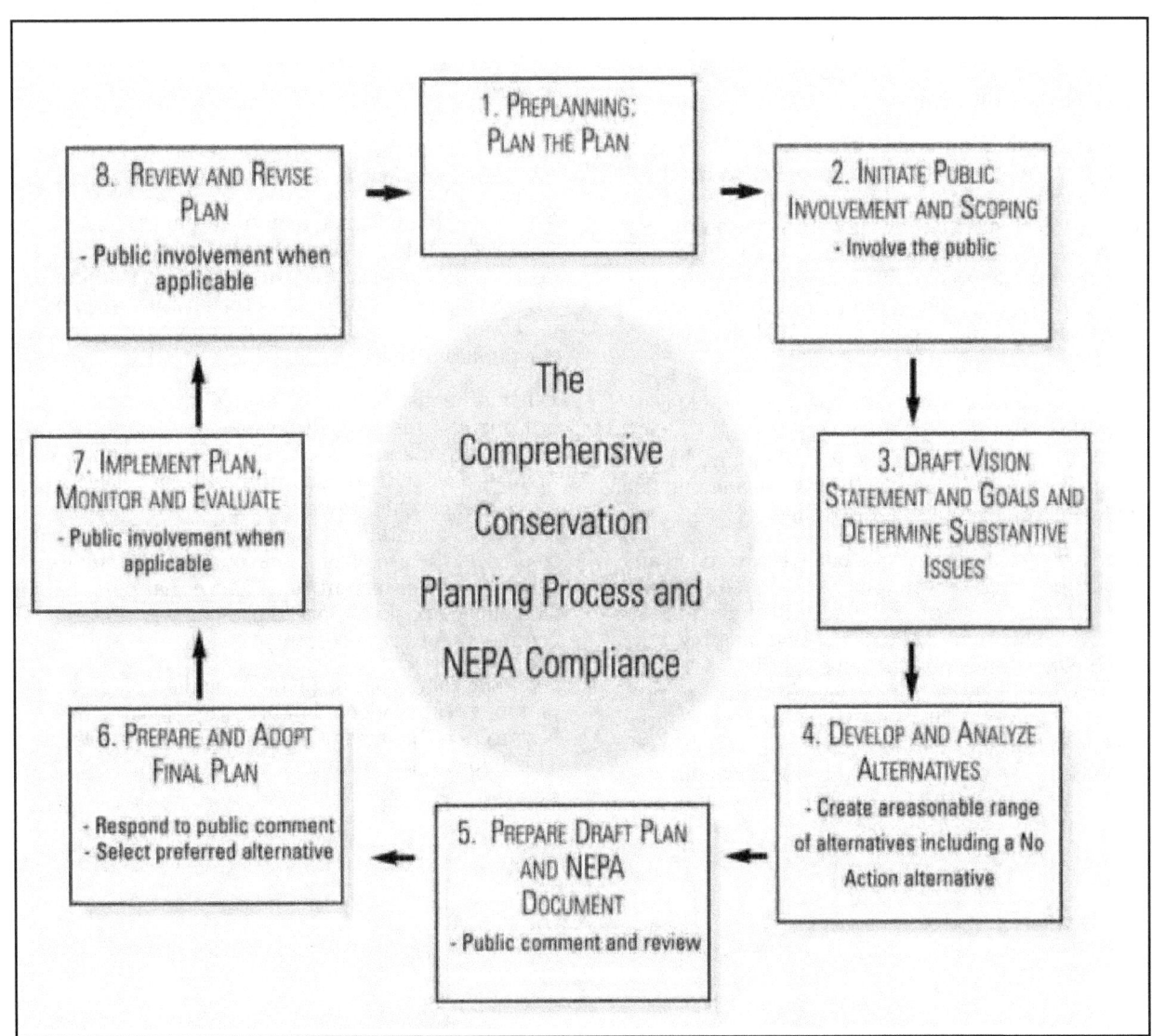

Figure 1. The steps in the CCP process

The Service began the pre-planning process in September 2004. A planning team comprised of Service personnel from the Lacreek National Wildlife Refuge (there are currently no Service personnel at the Bear Butte National Wildlife Refuge) was developed shortly after the initial kickoff meeting. The planning team developed issues and qualities lists. The refuge is part of the Lacreek National Wildlife Refuge Complex, headquartered near Martin, South Dakota.

A notice of intent was published in the "Federal Register" on November 30, 2004. Notification of a public open house was distributed through media press releases.

In October 2004, the region 6 regional director invited the director of the SDGFP to participate in the CCP. The local SDGFP wildlife managers and the Bear Butte State Park manager met with the refuge staff and planning team in early December to discuss the CCP process and the state park operations. They held a public meeting later that evening in Sturgis, South Dakota. The refuge manager has contacted the Bureau of Land Management and state park personnel throughout the course of the project.

The regional director also sent letters to twenty-four Native American tribal governments in the northern plains informing them of the upcoming CCP project and inviting them to serve on the core team. Representatives from the Rosebud Sioux and the Oglala Sioux tribes attended a public open house in Martin, South Dakota, on November 30, 2004, and provided input for the CCP planning team.

The refuge biologist attended a meeting in March 2005 that included all the tribal Game and Fish Departments in the Dakotas and Montana. The group had no objections to the state managing fish and wildlife resources on the refuge.

On April 9, 2005, the refuge biologist attended an annual meeting between the SDGFP and several tribes to discuss issues related to Bear Butte State Park and surrounding lands. At that meeting the biologist informed the tribes of the easement refuge that Lacreek has on Bear Butte Lake and the CCP process. There were approximately forty people in attendance representing three tribes from South Dakota (Standing Rock, Rosebud, and Pine Ridge) and the Northern Cheyenne

Sandhill Crane

© 2005 Laura Crawford Williams

tribe of Montana. Also, in attendance were a state legislator and four SDGFP representatives.

The biologist explained how the easement was acquired, what the easement allows the Service to do, and the cooperative agreement with the State. The biologist then presented the alternatives and asked for verbal and written comments, as part of the public outreach process for the CCP.

During the discussion, the biologist was asked how many acres around the lake, itself, are under the easement and what the divestiture would involve. Two individuals, representing distinct constituencies, indicated that they would like the Service to maintain the easement because they want to protect the area from development and believed retaining the easement could serve that purpose. The biologist asked them to provide written comments for the record.

Over the course of pre-planning and scoping, the planning team collected information about the resources of the refuge and the surrounding areas. This information is summarized in "Chapter 4, Affected Environment."

2 The Limited-interest Refuge

2 The Limited-interest Refuge

ESTABLISHMENT, ACQUISITION, AND MANAGEMENT HISTORY

The easement refuge is almost identical to other easements acquired during the 1930s that established the right to impound water and close the area to hunting. During this period, the United States faced the Depression, a massive drought, and declining waterfowl and wildlife populations. To address this problem, the federal government developed limited-interest refuges through easement agreements with private landowners and states. Originally, easements were purchased from private landowners; however, almost the entire refuge boundary under easement is now owned by the State. A small area within the refuge boundary is not owned by the State, but is also not under an easement.

CURRENT STATUS OF THE LIMITED-INTEREST REFUGE

The Bear Butte limited-interest refuge is currently owned and operated by the State as part of the Bear Butte State Park, which is part of the state park system. The butte, itself, is sacred to many American Indian tribes who come here to hold religious ceremonies. Mato Paha or "Bear Mountain" is the Lakota name for the site.

The butte is located on the east side of Highway 79. It is within the boundaries of Bear Butte State Park, but is not on the refuge. Visitors can learn the geological story of this almost-volcano, its role as a pioneer landmark, and its continuing role as a holy mountain and founding place of religion for several plains tribes when visiting the Bear Butte Education Center.

The butte has a 1.75-mile limestone-surface trail which ascends from the foot of Bear Butte to its 4,426 foot summit. It is designated a National Recreational Trail and is maintained by state park personnel. Visitors can view four states from the mountain's peak. The summit of the mountain is also the north end of the Centennial Trail that meanders through the east-central Black Hills and extends 111 miles south to Wind Cave National Park.

Bear Butte Lake is in the limited-interest refuge and is where the cooperative agreement is implemented. At this location the State manages a campground and picnic area. It provides opportunities for fishing, hiking, and horseback riding as part of the state park.

Red-winged Blackbird

© 2005 Laura Crawford Williams

Bear Butte State Park is home to a small herd of bison.

REFUGE PURPOSE

The purposes of the refuge are as follows:

Executive Order, August 26, 1935 "…as a refuge and breeding ground for migratory birds and other wildlife…".

Migratory Bird Conservation Act "…for use as an inviolate sanctuary, or for any other management purpose, for migratory birds."

In addition to the legal drivers listed above, the refuge was established because of the easement agreement established in the late 1930s. As part of the purpose of the refuge the easement reads, "The exclusive and perpetual right and easement to flood with water, and to maintain and operate a natural or artificial lake thereon or in connection with other land included in what is known as the Bear Butte Lake Project, and to raise the water level thereof by means of dams, dikes, fill, ditches, spillways and other structures, for water conservation, drought relief, and for migratory bird and wildlife conservation purposes and to operate upon said lands and waters and maintain a wildlife conservation demonstration unit and a closed refuge and reservation for migratory birds and other wildlife." It was stipulated that if the purposes for which the easement was granted were abandoned, the land would revert to the grantors or their successors.

COMPATIBILITY POLICY

Lands within the Refuge System are different from federal, multiple-use public lands, such as National

Forest System lands, in that they are closed to all public uses unless specifically and legally opened. The Improvement Act clearly establishes that wildlife conservation is the singular Refuge System mission. To ensure the primacy of the Refuge System's wildlife conservation mission, a compatibility policy was developed and placed into effect on November 17, 2000, (http://policy.fws.gov /library/00fr62457.pdf). The compatibility policy states that the Service will not initiate or permit a new use of a refuge or expand, renew, or extend an existing use of a refuge, unless the Service has determined that the use is a compatible use, and that use is not inconsistent with public safety.

A refuge use is defined as any activity on a refuge, except administrative or law enforcement activity, carried out by or under the direction of an authorized Service employee. Recreational uses, including all actions associated with a recreational use, refuge management, economic activities, or other use by the public, are considered to be refuge uses. Facilities and activities associated with recreational public uses, or where there is an economic benefit associated with a use, require compatibility determinations (CDs). Refuge management activities, such as invasive species control, prescribed fire, scientific monitoring, as well as the facilities for managing a refuge do not require CDs.

A compatible use is a proposed or existing wildlife-dependent recreational use, or any other use of a refuge that, based on sound professional judgment, will not materially interfere with, or detract from, the fulfillment of the Refuge System mission or the purposes of the refuge. Sound professional judgment is further defined as a decision that is consistent with principles of fish and wildlife management and administration, available science and resources, and adherence to law. The Service will secure public input throughout the CCP and CD processes.

CDs are written determinations signed and dated by the refuge manager and the refuge supervisor stating that a proposed or existing use of a refuge is, or is not, a compatible use. CDs are typically completed as part of the CCP or step-down management plan process. Draft CDs are open to public input and comment. Once a final CD is made by the refuge manager, it is not subject to administrative appeal.

The determination of appropriateness is the first step in deciding whether the Service will permit a proposed or existing use on a refuge. After the Service determines a use is appropriate, it must then determine that it is compatible, before allowing the use. The Improvement Act states that six wildlife-dependent recreation uses are the priority public uses of the Refuge System and, when compatible, have been determined to be appropriate by law. These six uses—hunting, fishing, wildlife observation and photography, and environmental education and interpretation—are to receive enhanced consideration in planning and management over all other general public uses of the Refuge System. Uses which are necessary for the safe, practical, and effective conduct of a priority public use are also appropriate.

Some recreational activities, while wholesome and enjoyable, are not dependent on the presence of fish and wildlife, nor are they dependent on the expectation of encountering fish and wildlife. Many of these nonwildlife-dependent recreational activities are often disruptive or harmful to fish, wildlife, or plants, or may interfere with the use and enjoyment of a refuge by others engaged in wildlife-dependent recreation. These uses may more appropriately be conducted on private land or other public lands not specifically dedicated for wildlife conservation.

A CD is not required when the Service does not have jurisdiction over the use. Jurisdiction is not to be viewed as what type of law enforcement

Bridge

Tom Koerner /USFWS

jurisdiction the Service has over the refuge (i.e., proprietary or concurrent); rather, it asks the question of whether the Service has the legal authority to prohibit a use.

Property rights that are not vested in the federal government must be recognized and allowed whether or not the use might be compatible. In these cases CDs should not be done because the finding is moot, and because the determination may be misinterpreted to mean an activity that otherwise would not be compatible is found to be compatible by "circumstances."

VISION AND GOALS

The planning team developed a vision and a set of goals for the refuge. The vision describes what the refuge will be, or what the Service hopes to do, and is based on the Refuge System mission and purposes of Bear Butte National Wildlife Refuge.

VISION

The refuge is located in the foothills of the Black Hills, adjacent to Bear Butte, a sacred site for several Northern Plains tribes. Management will work with partners to protect the cultural significance of the area and to maintain its natural resource values. Opportunities to enjoy wildlife-dependent recreation shall continue to be available to all visitors.

GOALS

The goals are descriptive, broad statements of desired future condition of the refuge. Four goals were identified for the refuge.

1. *Wildlife and Habitat Management:* Work with partners to maintain habitat for migratory birds and other wildlife.
2. *Public Use:* Work with partners to provide opportunities for quality wildlife-dependent recreation and to promote awareness of the area's resources.
3. *Cultural Resources:* Recognize the cultural significance and sacredness of the Bear Butte area to plains tribes.
4. *Partnerships:* Support existing partnerships that protect the cultural significance of the area, maintain natural resource values, and manage visitor use.

REFUGE AND RESOURCE DESCRIPTION

SPECIAL VALUES

During the vision and goals workshop, the planning team identified the outstanding qualities of the refuge. Qualities are the characteristics and features that are evident when a person visits the refuge.

The refuge is in a wide valley within the Black Hills region of South Dakota. Its proximity to Bear Butte, itself, and the associated view shed makes it an appealing place to look at the butte from a distance.

Some of the structures at the refuge are part of the Depression-era programs designed by President Franklin D. Roosevelt to rebuild the country's resources. Remnants of that era can be found in the campground, including a former bathhouse, a picnic shelter, stone walls and the dam structure.

Bear Butte NWR

Tom Koerner/USFWS

Although no longer running, an artesian well fed the Bear Butte Lake and was once a unique and special value on the refuge.

ISSUES

Prior to writing the draft CCP, Service staff and other planning team members met to identify any significant issues that should be addressed in the plan. A public open house, news releases in the local and regional press, an announcement in the *Federal Register*, and numerous mailings were conducted to solicit public input on important issues to be addressed. Following are the most significant issues identified.

Habitat and Wildlife

The Service acquired a limited-interest easement to flood with water and to maintain and operate a natural or artificial lake for migratory birds and conservation purposes. However, from the beginning Bear Butte NWR was developed more as a recreation area with many non-wildlife dependent public use facilities such as a beach, swimming pond, boat ramps and campground and picnic areas. The inviolate sanctuary provisions of the refuge's purpose have never been enforced and, as a result, a loss of biodiversity and wildlife habitat has occurred. Therefore, the Service does not manage habitat and wildlife because the refuge is used for other recreation purposes.

Public Use

The Improvement Act recognized that wildlife-dependent recreational uses—hunting, fishing, wildlife observation and photography, and environmental education and interpretation—when determined to be compatible are legitimate and appropriate public uses of a refuge; however, the Service believes that the types of public use that occur at the refuge create too much disturbance to provide a sanctuary for migratory birds.

From the beginning, one of the primary purposes intended for the Bear Butte area was recreation. As mentioned earlier, a number of facilities were constructed at about the same time as the dam, to encourage and support camping, swimming, boating, and picnicking. There is little evidence that the inviolate sanctuary provisions of the refuge's purpose were ever enforced.

The Service also has the right to close the area to hunting and current state park regulations allow hunting on the refuge.

Water Management

The Bear Butte Lake Project created an artificial lake which raised water levels by means of an earthen dam and spillway. Originally the lake was filled by an artesian well; however, it stopped flowing and was plugged by the State in May 1987. The water levels are now completely dependent on annual rainfall. The watershed for this lake is relatively small compared to its size. Without supplemental flows of the artesian well, the water levels of the lake have remained low. The Service does not perform any water management activities on the refuge.

Cultural Resources

The refuge staff recognizes the importance of the cultural resources at the refuge to the Native American community. The Service does not manage any cultural resources in the state park or refuge.

Administration

Limited management activities by the Service have occurred at the refuge. As a limited-interest refuge, the Service entered into a cooperative agreement with the State, which made the State responsible for administering, operating and maintaining the refuge. Conflicting uses of the refuge as a state park versus a national wildlife refuge creates a problem for the Service to fully implement the refuge's purpose.

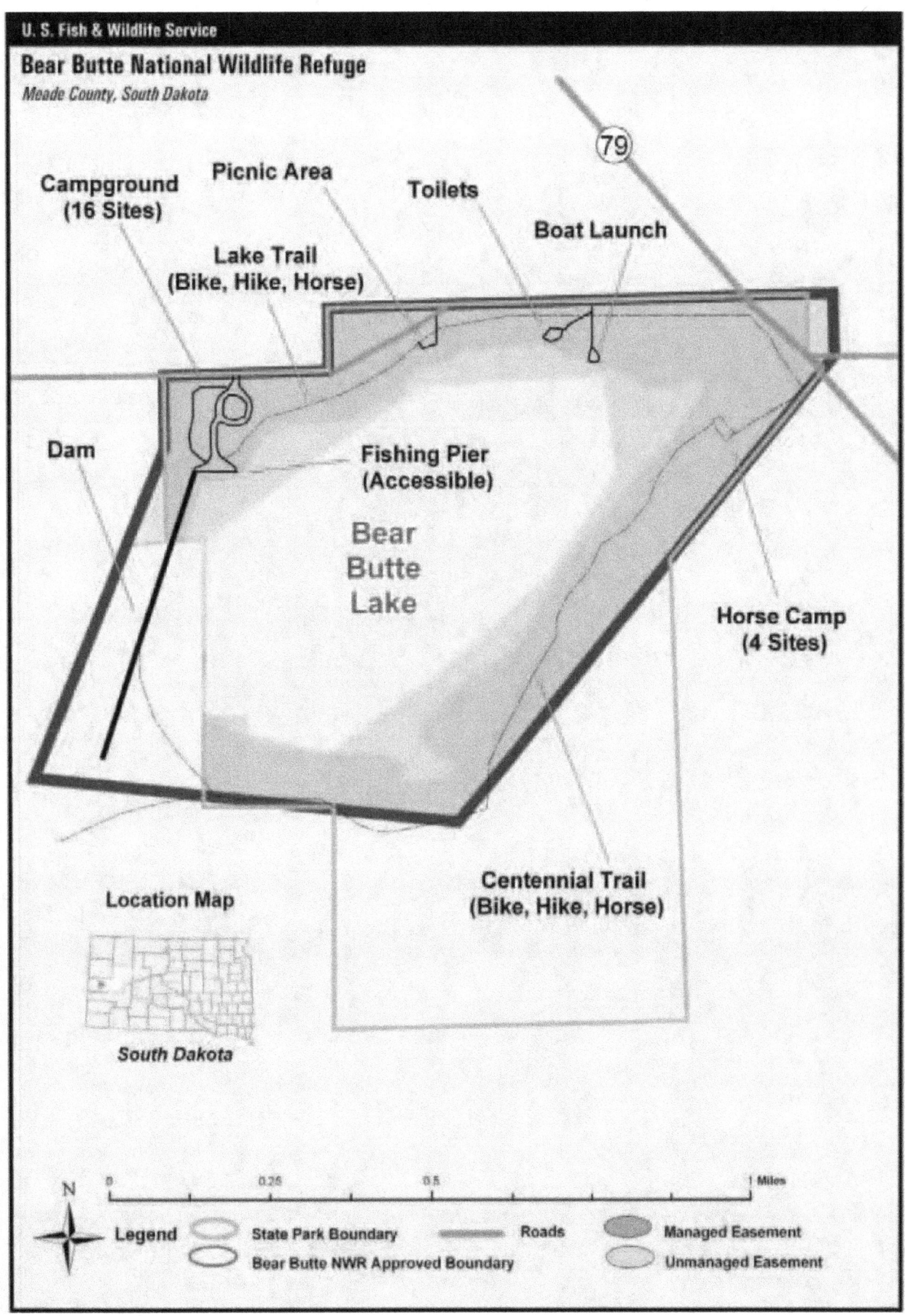

Figure 2. Location Map

3 Alternatives

Great Blue Heron
Tom Kelley/USFWS

3 Alternatives

INTRODUCTION

Alternatives are different approaches to management of the refuge. They are designed to resolve issues, achieve the refuge purpose, vision, and goals as identified in the CCP, and fulfill the mission of the Refuge System. They must also comply with current laws, regulations, and policies. NEPA requires an equal and full analysis of all alternatives considered for implementation.

In fall 2004 the Service held a meeting with the public to identify the issues and concerns that were associated with the management of the refuge. The public involvement process is summarized in greater detail in chapter 2. Based on public input, as well as guidelines from NEPA, the Improvement Act, and Service planning policy, the planning team selected the substantive issues that will be addressed in the alternatives. Substantive issues identified for the refuge are:

1. habitat and wildlife management
2. public use
3. water management
4. management activities
5. cultural resources

The planning team discussed alternatives for management that will address the substantive refuge issues and meet the goals of the Refuge System. Each alternative described in the following sections addresses the substantive issues somewhat differently.

This chapter describes two management alternatives for the refuge: Alternative A, Current Management (no action); Alternative B, Relinquish Easement to Current Landowners (Proposed Action).

ALTERNATIVES CONSIDERED BUT ELIMINATED FROM DETAILED STUDY

One alternative the planning team considered would increase the Service's management activities at the refuge. This alternative was rejected because current management of the refuge is provided by the SDGFP, and the area is currently managed as a state park. Increased management by Service personnel would conflict with the State's ability to administer, operate, and maintain the area as they have been doing under the cooperative agreement since 1967.

This alternative was also eliminated from further study because Service personnel determined that it is not feasible to maintain the refuge's habitat alongside the recreational uses (e.g., camping and picnicking) that occur at the park.

The other alternative considered but eliminated from further study was to transfer the easement to another entity. Under the provisions of the easement agreements, however, the Service cannot turn over the easement to any party except the current landowners.

DESCRIPTION OF ALTERNATIVES

The theme and general management direction for each alternative are described below.

ALTERNATIVE A—CURRENT MANAGEMENT (NO ACTION)

Alternative A, the no-action alternative, describes current and future management of the refuge. It provides the baseline against which to compare the proposed action. It is also a requirement of NEPA that the no-action alternative be addressed.

Under the no-action alternative, the Service would continue to manage the refuge within the parameters of the cooperative agreement with the SDGFP. Existing habitat within the easement and all public programs would continue to be administered and maintained by the State.

Current habitat and wildlife practices would be carried out by park personnel and levels of public use would remain the same. The park facilities and activities—hiking, picnicking, designated camping, fishing, and a horse camp—that are provided on the southeast side of Bear Butte Lake would continue to be offered.

Refuge staff would support partnerships between the State and the tribes for the ongoing protection of cultural resources. The Service would continue passive management and maintenance of facilities (no refuge staff is currently assigned to the station).

ALTERNATIVE B—PROPOSED ACTION (RELINQUISH EASEMENT TO CURRENT LANDOWNERS)

Alternative B, the proposed action, would take the refuge out of the Refuge System and relinquish the easement to the current landowners. Under this alternative, the habitat, public use, cultural resources and operations would be managed by the landowners. The Service's easement requirements would no longer exist.

The Service would divest its interest in the refuge. This would be carried out within the life of the plan. Once the CCP is approved, the managing station would work with the division of realty and the land protection planning branch within the division of refuge planning to prepare a combined program proposal to divest this refuge. The proposal would be submitted to the Migratory Bird Conservation Commission for concurrence and then submitted for congressional approval.

COMPARISON OF ALTERNATIVES

The two alternatives evaluated in this planning process are (1) no action and (2) relinquish the Services interest to current landowners. A comparison of the alternatives is shown in table 1.

Bear Butte State Park

Table 1. Comparison of the alternatives

Issue	Alternative A (No Action)	Alternative B (Relinquish Easement to Current Landowners*)
Habitat and Wildlife	Passive management; maintain existing habitat with easement	The landowners have sole responsibility to manage habitat and wildlife
Public Use	Continue to allow the State, the Bureau of Land Management, and private landowner to manage all public-use programs	Same as A
Cultural Resources	Support partnerships between the State and the tribes for the ongoing protection of cultural resources	The landowners have sole responsibility to protect cultural resources
Operations and Maintenance	Passive management and no maintenance	The landowners are responsible for operations and maintenance
Partnerships	Continue to work with State, tribal, and federal partners	Continue to work with State, tribal, and federal partners
Easement Rights	Maintain the right to impound water	All easement rights, including the right to impound water, will be voluntarily relinquished to the State

The SDGFP and other current landowners

4 Affected Environment

GENERAL OVERVIEW OF REFUGE

The refuge is six miles northeast of Sturgis, South Dakota and is part of the Lacreek National Wildlife Refuge Complex headquartered in Martin, South Dakota. The refuge is within the boundary of Bear Butte State Park and is managed by the SDGFP. Sacred to the plains Indian tribes, the butte, itself, is the place where the god, Maheo imparted to Sweet Medicine (a mythical hero) the knowledge from which the Cheyenne derive their religious, political, social, and economic customs. The butte site is a national natural and historic landmark. It is within the boundaries of Bear Butte State Park but is not on the refuge.

PHYSICAL ENVIRONMENT

AIR QUALITY

The National Ambient Air Quality Standards include maximum allowable pollution levels for particulate matter (a measure of microscopic liquid or solid particles that is respirable in the lungs), ozone, sulfur dioxide, nitrogen dioxide, lead, and carbon dioxide.

Air quality in the area of the refuge is considered good, with no nearby manufacturing sites or major air pollution sources. Carbon from automobiles and diesel engines, prescribed fire activities on the refuge, and dust associated with wind-blown sand and dirt from the roadways and fields contribute to particulate matter.

CLIMATE

January and February are the coldest months of winter. Late winter and early spring is western South Dakota's snow season. March is typically the snowiest month of the year.

Late spring is western South Dakota's rainy season, when the area receives over a third of its annual moisture. Precipitation in May comes mostly in showers. By June, thunderstorms are a common occurrence. June marks the peak of severe weather season.

Mid-summer around the Black Hills is warm and dry with plenty of sunshine. Sporadic thunderstorms are an almost-daily summertime occurrence over the Black Hills during the afternoon and evening. They usually produce only brief showers. Rainfall decreases as summer draws to a close.

Sunny, mild days and cool nights are typical during the months of September and October. The average

Mink

first freeze occurs sometime between late August and September in the Black Hills. Winter weather starts sometime between November and December in the Black Hills. Snowfall averages about 5 inches each month, but most snow is light, as a typical month has only 2 days when more than 1 inch of snow falls.

PHYSIOGRAPHIC, GEOGRAPHY, AND SOILS

Bear Butte is a laccolith located in the Black Hills, an area of uplifted Precambrian on the Wyoming–South Dakota state line. Bear Butte is made of magma that never reached the surface to generate an eruption. The magma intruded to a shallow level and then stopped, cooled, crystallized, and solidified. Erosion then stripped the overlying layers of rock away. Bear Butte is at the east end of a linear belt of volcanic centers that continues westward about 60 miles to Devils Tower. The rock is called a trachyte based on its mineral composition, which includes alkali feldspar, with small amounts of biotite, hornblende, and pyroxene. Bear Butte rises 1,253 feet above the surrounding plain.

WATER RESOURCES

The Bear Butte Lake Project created the limited-interest refuge around Bear Butte Lake. It was a natural lake enhanced through the construction of a dam to capture runoff. An easement was established for the use of all water from an artesian well which has since stopped flowing, and was abandoned by the State in May 1987. The SDGFP holds Water License #844-1 for 520 cubic feet-per-second from dry draws to stabilize Bear Butte Lake levels for recreational purposes (priority date 4/12/1968).

BIOLOGICAL RESOURCES

This section describes the existing and potential plant and animal communities in the refuge.

HABITATS

The refuge's habitats are comprised of mixed-grass prairie in the uplands with a very rapid transition to a lacustrine, or lake habitat, in the permanently impounded area within the high-water mark behind the dam. The plant community of the mixed-grass prairie is greatly influenced by precipitation and the great annual variability that occurs here. The tall-grass prairies to the east receive greater annual precipitation while the short-grass prairies to the west receive less. The plant community of the mixed-grass prairie reflects this, with species from both the tall- and short-grass prairies found here. Grasses dominate the uplands, including the native, cool season species of western wheatgrass (*Pascopyrum smithii*), green needlegrass (*Stipa viridula*), and needle and thread grass (*Stipa comata*). Exotic cool-season grasses, including smooth bromegrass (*Bromus inermis*), Kentucky bluegrass (*Poa pratensis*), and crested wheatgrass (*Agropyron cristatum*) have invaded the site, and make up a significant portion of the plant community. The remainder of the plant community is made up of smaller percentages of the following: slender wheatgrass (*Agropyron caninum*), bluebunch wheatgrass (*Agropyron spicatum*), barnyard grass (*Echinochloa crusgalli*), little bluestem (*Schizachyrium scoparium*), foxtail barley (*Hordeum jubatum*), June grass (*Koeleria pyramidata*), marsh muhly (*Muhlenbergia racemosa*), roughleaf ricegrass (*Oryzopsis asperifolia*), Indian ricegrass (*Oryzopsis hymenoides*), western wheatgrass (*Pascopyrum smithii*), Timothy (*Phleum pratense*), Canada bluegrass (*Poa compressa*), Canby's bluegrass (*Poa canbyi*), inland bluegrass (*Poa interior*), squirreltail (*Sitanion hystrix*), needle-and-thread grass *(Stipa comata)*, and porcupine grass *(Stipa spartea)*.

The lake portion is primarily a deep-water habitat, supporting little to no emergent wetland vegetation.

AQUATIC HABITAT

The refuge provides aquatic habitat for a range of plants and animals. Western painted turtles, blotched tiger salamander, and the upland chorus frog are found on the refuge. A variety of snakes including the western plains and wandering garter snake are found near water. The eastern yellow-bellied racer, bullsnake, and prairie rattlesnake are abundant.

BIRDS

Bird populations on the refuge are dependent on the use and availability of natural resources, including water levels on the lake. Documentation of bird occurrence and use is not well-developed for this refuge. Water birds seen on the refuge include: American white pelicans, western grebes, double-crested cormorants, Canada and snow geese, mallards, blue-winged and green-winged teals. Birds of prey seen on the refuge include Swainson's and red-tailed hawks and American kestrel. Shorebirds include kildeer, lesser yellowlegs, and upland sandpipers. Sharp-tailed grouse, American coot, burrowing owls, and black-billed magpie are also seen on the refuge. A complete list of birds that occur on the refuge is in appendix B.

FISH

Bear Butte Lake has a surface area of 180 acres and a maximum depth of 13 feet. The lake is owned and managed by the SDGFP. Currently there are four primary game and forage and four secondary species of fish that occur in the lake. Primary game fish are largemouth bass, yellow perch, black crappie and

Canada Geese Taking Flight

northern pike. Secondary species are green sunfish, fathead minnow rock bass and black bullhead.

MAMMALS

Mammals that occur on the refuge include the common raccoon, black-tailed prairie dog, northern pocket gopher, deer mouse, eastern cottontail and whitetail deer, and bison.

THREATENED AND ENDANGERED SPECIES

Bald eagles are common winter residents on the refuge and within the state park. Previously listed as endangered, their status was upgraded to threatened in July 1995. The bald eagle is also listed as a state-threatened species. Whooping cranes occur in Meade County, but because of boating on the lake and other uses in the campground, they are not likely to be found on the refuge.

CULTURAL RESOURCES

The region is sacred to Native Americans of the plains who consider The Black Hills to be the Axis Mundi, the center of the world.

Bear Butte's geological feature was an important landmark and religious site for plains Indian tribes dating back 10,000 years, well before Europeans reached South Dakota, and it continues to be today. Bear Butte is called Mato Paha or "Bear Mountain" by the Lakota. To the Cheyenne, it is Noahvose. The mountain is sacred to many indigenous peoples, who make pilgrimages to pray and leave prayer ties on the branches of trees along the trail that leads to the top of the butte.

Notable leaders including, Red Cloud, Crazy Horse and Sitting Bull, have all visited Bear Butte. These visits culminated with an 1857 gathering of many Native American nations to discuss the advancement of white settlers into the Black Hills.

George A. Custer, who led an expedition of 1,000 men into the region, camped near the mountain. Custer verified the rumors of gold in the Black Hills. Bear Butte then served as a landmark that helped guide the rush of invading prospectors and settlers into the region.

SPECIAL MANAGEMENT AREAS

WILDERNESS

To be designated a wilderness area, lands must meet certain criteria as outlined in the Wilderness Act of 1964:

- Generally appear to have been affected primarily by the forces of nature, with the imprint of human work substantially unnoticeable;
- Have outstanding opportunities for solitude, or a primitive and unconfined type of recreation;

- Have at least 5,000 acres of land, or be of sufficient size as to make practicable its preservation and use in an unimpaired condition, and;
- May also contain ecological, geological, or other features of scientific, educational, scenic, or historical value.

Bear Butte National Wildlife Refuge does not meet the criteria for a wilderness area.

The butte, itself, was placed on the National Register of Historic Places in 1973 and became a national natural landmark in 1965. The National Natural Landmarks Program recognizes and encourages the conservation of outstanding examples of our country's natural history. It is the only natural areas program of national scope that identifies and recognizes the best examples of biological and geological features in both public and private ownership.

The trail leading to the summit is designated a national recreation trail. As part of the George S. Mickelson Trail which spans 114 miles across four counties, this "crown jewel" of the state park system provides a unique educational and recreational experience for visitors of all ages. Winding through the heart of the Black Hills utilizing numerous bridges and tunnels, this rail-trail brings to life the area's rich history with stories of American Indians, miners, railroad workers, and many others.

Due to the configuration of the refuge within the state park, it does not have these designations as a national register property, national natural landmark, or a national recreation trail.

VISITOR SERVICES

Because the refuge is located within Bear Butte State Park, a number of park facilities exist. The park offers a hiking trail around Bear Butte Lake, sixteen nonelectric campsites, fishing for bullheads, crappies and northern pike, and the use of boats with 25-horsepower or smaller motors. There is a wheelchair-accessible fishing dock. A horse camp is provided on the southeast side of the lake. Two miles of natural trail exists around Bear Butte Lake; however, horseback riding is only allowed west of Highway 79. The trail connects to Centennial Trail, which leads riders through the Black Hills. The horse camp with primitive sites, water, and corral is available on a first-come, first-served basis only. Hunting, especially deer and waterfowl, is very popular in the area. The State does not allow hunting in some sections of the park. Uncased firearms and bows are prohibited year-round in the designated campground and within the park east of Highway 79.

SOCIOECONOMIC ENVIRONMENT

This section characterizes current socioeconomic conditions in Meade County, South Dakota.

Bear Butte is located in Meade County, South Dakota. According to the 2000 census, the county has a population of 24,253—8,805 households and 6,700 families. The average household size is 2.66 and the average family size is 3.05. The racial makeup of the county is 92.65% white, 2.10% Hispanic or Latino, 2.04% Native American, 1.48% black or African American, 0.63% Asian, 0.07% Pacific Islander, 0.61% from other races, and 2.52% from two or more races. According to the 2000 census, educational, health and social services are the largest industries, followed by retail-trade arts, entertainment, recreation, accommodation, and food services. The median family income is $40,537 per year.

Hard-surfaced state and federal highways bisect the county in both north-south and east-west directions.

Sturgis is the nearest city to the state park and the refuge. As of the 2000 census, the city had a total population of 6,442. The median income for a household in the city is $30,253 and the median income for a family is $38,698. The racial make up is similar to the rest of the county.

Picnic Shelter

Tom Koerner / USFWS

Every August the city hosts one of the largest annual motorcycle events in the world. The campground at Bear Butte State Park is used by motorcycle enthusiast during the motorcycle rally. The number of campground and state park users increase during this period.

5 Environmental Consequences

Flax
Shapins Associates

5 Environmental Consequences

This section analyzes and discusses the potential environmental effects or consequences that can be expected by the implementation of each management alternative described in chapter 3. Table 2 gives a comparison of the environmental consequences of each alternative.

EFFECTS COMMON TO ALL ALTERNATIVES

ENVIRONMENTAL JUSTICE

Environmental justice refers to the principle that all citizens and communities are entitled to:

- equal protection from environmental, occupational health, or safety hazards;
- equal access to natural resources, and;
- equal participation in the environmental and natural resource policy formulation process.

On February 11, 1994, President Clinton issued EO 12898: Federal Actions to Address Environmental Justice in Minority Populations and Income Populations. The purpose of this order is to focus the attention of federal agencies on human environmental health and to address inequities that may occur in the distribution of: costs and benefits, land-use patterns, hazardous material transport or facility siting, allocation and consumption of resources, access to information, planning, and decision making.

Within the spirit and intent of EO 12898, no minority or low-income populations would be impacted by any Service action under the two alternatives presented in this document.

SOCIOECONOMIC IMPACTS

Economic impacts are typically measured in terms of number of jobs lost or gained and the associated result on income. Neither alternative would significantly impact the economics of the local area.

CUMULATIVE IMPACTS

Cumulative impacts are the potential effects of the action or no-action alternatives in combination with past, present, and future actions. NEPA regulations define cumulative effects "as the impact on the environment which results from the incremental impact of the action when added to other past, present, and reasonably foreseeable future actions regardless of what agency (federal or nonfederal) or person undertakes such other actions. Cumulative impacts can result from individually minor, but collectively significant, actions taking place over time." (40 Code of Federal Regulations 1508.7.)

The cumulative effects analysis for this project is based on reasonably foreseeable future actions that, if implemented, would contribute to the effects of the action or no-action alternative. No reasonably foreseeable actions are anticipated.

EFFECTS OF ALTERNATIVE A

Under the no-action alternative, the Service would continue to manage the refuge within the parameters of the cooperative agreement with the SDGFP. Existing habitat within the easement and all public programs would continue to be administered and maintained by the State.

HABITATS AND WILDLIFE

Under alternative A, the refuge would maintain the current habitat management program administered through the cooperative agreement with the State. The uplands and wetlands would be managed as part of the state park, and passive management of the existing habitat within the easement would continue giving the refuge staff little ability to promote species diversity.

Because of multiple uses and alterations of the landscape and the size and connectivity of habitat patches, which makes movement of wildlife or genetic information between parcels of land difficult or impossible, the habitat can no longer support species diversity.

WATER MANAGEMENT

The water cycle on Bear Butte Lake under both alternatives would continue to be dependent on spring runoff and annual rainfall. The ability to hold water levels and wetland conditions through water management would continue to be dependent on annual precipitation. Water cycle conditions will have little to no effect on current bird populations. There would be no change in existing water-quality conditions and sedimentation trends.

PUBLIC USE

All public programs are administered by the State under alternative A. Conflicting purposes of the State and the Service do not allow the Service to provide opportunities for the six priority public-use activities. The state, for example, provides campgrounds within the refuge boundary. Campgrounds are not a priority use on refuges nor are they wildlife compatible or wildlife dependent, and as such are generally not allowed. In a few situations they are allowed to support priority public uses, but in this case camping does not support these uses.

Current on- and off-refuge opportunities for wildlife viewing, education, and interpretation would be retained. This includes informational kiosks, hiking trails, day-use areas, a fishing platform, and educational programs. These programs would continue to place an emphasis on the state park and its programs. Visitors would not be aware that they are visiting a refuge.

Under alternative A, there would be no change in current management of hunting and fishing opportunities.

CULTURAL RESOURCES

Under alternative A, there would be no changes to cultural resource management. Current management activities would continue to be carried out solely by the State under the cooperative agreement.

OPERATIONS AND MAINTENANCE

Under alternative A, there would be no change in current operations and maintenance activities.

SOCIOECONOMIC IMPACTS

Under alternative A, there would be no change in socioeconomic climate.

EFFECTS OF ALTERNATIVE B

Under alternative B, the proposed action would take the refuge out of the Refuge System and the easement would be transferred to the State. Under this alternative, the habitat, public use, cultural resources, and operations would be managed by the landowners. The Service's easement requirements would no longer exist. The Service would divest its interest in the refuge.

HABITATS AND WILDLIFE

Since the State currently maintains habitats and wildlife, there would be no change. The cooperative agreement would no longer be in place and easement would be removed.

WATER MANAGEMENT

Since the State is currently responsible for water issues, there would be no change. The cooperative agreement would no longer be in place and easement would be removed.

PUBLIC USE

Since the State is currently responsible for issues relating to public use, there would be no change. The cooperative agreement would no longer be in place and easement would be removed.

CULTURAL RESOURCES

Since the State is currently responsible for issues relating to cultural resources, there would be no change. The cooperative agreement would no longer be in place and easement would be removed.

OPERATIONS AND MAINTENANCE

Since the State is currently responsible for operations and maintenance, there would be no change. The cooperative agreement would no longer be in place and easement would be removed.

SOCIOECONOMIC IMPACTS

Since there will be no change to the aforementioned categories, there should not be any change to the socioeconomic impact.

Table 2. Description of consequences by alternative

Issue	Alternative A (no action)	Alternative B (proposed action)
Habitats and Wildlife	Continued reliance on State to manage habitats and wildlife.	Same as A except cooperative agreement would no longer be in place and easement would be removed.
Water Management	Continued dependence on annual rainfall. Continued emphasis on providing recreational activities. No change in existing water-quality conditions and sedimentation trends.	Same as A except cooperative agreement would no longer be in place and easement would be removed.
Public Use	Review existing nonwildlife-dependent recreation uses for compliance with the Improvement Act and accompanying regulations and policies through a CD process.	Current public-use activities, including nonwildlife-dependent activities, would continue. Non compliance with Improvement Act would no longer be an issue.
Cultural Resources	The State would continue to manage the cultural resources.	Same as A except cooperative agreement would no longer be in place.
Operations and Maintenance	Continue current level of operations and maintenance under cooperative agreement.	Current operations and maintenance activities would continue.
Socioeconomic Impacts	No change to socioeconomic climate.	No change to socioeconomic climate.

6 Management Direction

6 Management Direction

It is the responsibility of the planning team to recommend a proposed action that best achieves the planning unit purposes, vision, and goals and helps fulfill the Refuge System mission. Once the preferred management alternative has been selected and finalized, the CCP has been approved, and the Service has notified the public of its decision, the implementation phase of the CCP begins.

MANAGEMENT SUMMARY

Alternative B, the proposed action, would take the refuge out of the Refuge System and transfer the easement to the current landowner. Under this alternative, the landowners would manage the habitat, public use, cultural resources, and operations. The Service would divest its interest in the refuge. This would be carried out within the 15-year life of the plan.

MANAGEMENT DIRECTION

Within 5 years of CCP approval, the Service would relinquish the refuge to the current landowners to

Bear Butte Lake

Tom Koerner / USFWS

provide all services and activities related to habitat, public use, cultural resources and partnerships.

The Service would work with the State to divest the Service's interest. It would revoke the refuge and flowage easement agreements, transferring full control to the current landowners.

Because the interests of the State and the Refuge System are not compatible, and because the State has maintained the refuge since 1967, the Service believes it makes sense to divest itself.

The refuge was established in 1937 as an easement refuge on and around Bear Butte Lake. The refuge was established for the purpose of water conservation, drought relief, and migratory bird and wildlife conservation purposes. Following establishment, however, incompatible uses such as boating, camping, picnicking have been permitted and supported. During the period when the dam was constructed, the CCC and WPA also built recreation facilities to support these and other uses.

The Service believes that some recreational activities, while wholesome and enjoyable, are not dependent on the presence of fish and wildlife, nor dependent on the expectation of encountering fish and wildlife. Many of these nonwildlife-dependent recreational activities are often disruptive or harmful to fish, wildlife, or plants, or may interfere with the use and enjoyment of a refuge by others engaged in wildlife-dependent recreation. These uses may more appropriately be conducted on private land, or other public lands not specifically dedicated for wildlife conservation. Because wildlife conservation is the singular Refuge System mission, the Service believes it is both feasible and necessary to turn over its interest in the resource to the current landowners.

Through the CCP process the Service evaluated the level of trust-resource value to determine if those values and associated risks to those values are sufficient to justify continuation of the easement. Trust resources are resources that through law or administrative act are held in trust for the people by the government. The Service recognizes that because the refuge is operated by the State as a state park, many actions that may be enforced for wildlife conservation cannot be implemented. Almost all of the subject lands and waters would be provided some protection without the Services easement and the State would continue to manage the habitat, public use, cultural resources and operate the refuge as part of Bear Butte State Park.

Partnerships with state, tribal and local entities would continue.

The planning division of the Service's regional office brought together refuge managers, supervisors, a regional biologist, planners, realty staff, and the senior management team to develop a model that asks a series of questions to help the Service determine whether or not a refuge should remain part of the Refuge System. The model was designed for field-level refuge staff to use during the preplanning process for a CCP. The Bear Butte National Wildlife Refuge did not pass the test to remain as a refuge in the Refuge System. The results are in appendix E.

Glossary

Canada Goose
Bob Savannah/USFWS

alternative: (1) A reasonable way to solve an identified problem or satisfy the stated need (40 CFR 1500.2). (2) Alternatives are different means of accomplishing refuge purposes and goals and contributing to the Refuge System mission (Draft Service Manual 602 FW 1.5).

CCP: See comprehensive conservation plan.

biological integrity: Biotic composition, structure and function at genetic, organism and community levels comparable with historic conditions, including the natural biological processes that shape the genomes, organisms, and communities.

compatible use: A wildlife-dependent recreational use or any other use of a refuge that, in the sound professional judgment of the director of the U.S. Fish and Wildlife Service, will not materially interfere with or detract from the fulfillment of the mission of the Refuge System or the purposes of the refuge (Draft Service Manual 603 FW 3.6). A compatibility determination supports the selection of compatible uses and identified stipulations or limits necessary to ensure compatibility.

comprehensive conservation plan (CCP): A document that describes the desired future conditions of the refuge; and provides long-range guidance and management direction for the refuge manager to accomplish the purposes of the refuge, contribute to the mission of the Refuge System, and to meet other relevant mandates (Draft Service Manual 602 FW 1.5).

cultural resources: The remains of sites, structures, or objects used by people in the past.

easement refuge: See limited-interest national wildlife refuge.

ecosystem: A dynamic and interrelating complex of plant and animal communities and their associated non-living environment. A biological community, together with its environment, functioning as a unit. For administrative purposes, the Service has designated fifty-three ecosystems covering the United States and its possessions. These ecosystems generally correspond with watershed boundaries and their sizes and ecological complexity vary.

endangered species (federal): A plant or animal species listed under the Endangered Species Act of 1973 (as amended) that is in danger of extinction throughout all, or a significant portion of, its range.

endangered species (state): A plant or animal species in danger of becoming extinct or extirpated in a particular state within the near future if factors contributing to its decline continue. Populations of these species are at critically low levels or their habitats have been degraded or depleted to a significant degree.

environmental assessment (EA): A concise public document, prepared in compliance with the National Environmental Policy Act, that briefly discusses the purpose and need for an action, alternatives to such action, and provides sufficient evidence and analysis of impacts to determine whether to prepare an Environmental Impact Statement or Finding of No Significant Impact (40 CFR 1508.9).

fragmentation: The alteration of a large block of habitat which creates isolated patches of the original habitat that are interspersed with a variety of other habitat types (Koford et al. 1994); the process of reducing the size and connectivity of habitat patches, making movement of individuals or genetic information between parcels difficult or impossible.

goal: Descriptive, open-ended, and often broad statement of desired future conditions that conveys a purpose but does not define measurable units (Draft Service Manual 620 FW 1.5).

habitat: Suite of existing environmental conditions required by an organism for survival and reproductions. The place where an organism typically lives and grows.

habitat disturbance: Significant alteration of habitat structure or composition. Event may be natural (e.g., fire) or human-caused (e.g., timber harvest, disking).

habitat type (vegetation type, cover type): A land classification system based on the concept of distinct plant associations.

impoundment: A body of water created by collection and confinement within a series of levees or dikes thus creating separate management units although not always independent of one another.

inviolate sanctuary: A place of refuge or protection where animals and birds may not be hunted.

invasive plant: a species that is non-native to the ecosystem under consideration and whose introduction causes, or is likely to cause, economic or environmental harm or harm to human health.

issue: Any unsettled matter that requires a management decision; e.g., a Service initiative, opportunity, resource management problem, a threat to the resources of the unit, conflict in uses, public concern, or the presence of an undesirable resource condition (Draft Service Manual 602 FW 1.5).

limited-interest national wildlife refuge: a national wildlife refuge which has more than 85% of its approved boundary covered by a 1930s flowage easement and/or refuge easement, giving the Service limited management capabilities.

management alternative: See alternative.

migration: Regular extensive, seasonal movements of birds between their breeding regions and their "wintering" regions (Koford et al. 1994); to pass periodically from one region or climate to another for feeding or breeding.

migratory birds: Birds which follow a seasonal movement from their breeding grounds to their "wintering" grounds. Waterfowl, shorebirds, raptors, and song birds are all migratory birds.

mission: Succinct statement of purpose and/or reason for being.

mixed-grass prairie: A transition zone between the tall-grass prairie and the short-grass prairie dominated by grasses of medium height that are approximately 2–4 feet tall. Soils are not as rich as the tall-grass prairie and moisture levels are less.

national wildlife refuge: "A designated area of land, water, or an interest in land or water within the Refuge System, but does not include coordination areas." Find a complete listing of all units of the Refuge System in the current *Annual Report of Lands Under Control of the U.S. Fish and Wildlife Service.*

National Wildlife Refuge System: Various categories of areas administered by the Secretary of the Interior for the conservation of fish and wildlife, including species threatened with extinction, all lands, waters, and interests therein administered by the Secretary as wildlife refuges, areas for the protection and conservation of fish and wildlife that are threatened with extinction, wildlife ranges, game ranges, wildlife management areas, or waterfowl production areas.

National Wildlife Refuge System Improvement Act of 1997: Sets the mission and the administrative policy for all refuges in the Refuge System. Clearly defines a unifying mission for the Refuge System; establishes the legitimacy and appropriateness of the six priority public uses (hunting, fishing, wildlife observation and photography, and environmental education and interpretation); establishes a formal process for determining appropriateness and compatibility; establish the responsibilities of the Secretary of the Interior for managing and protecting the Refuge System; and requires a comprehensive conservation plan for each refuge by the year 2012. This Act amended portions of the Refuge Recreation Act and National Wildlife Refuge System Administration Act of 1966.

native species: A species that occurred or currently occurs in that ecosystem and is not the result of human introduction into that ecosystem.

nongovernmental organization: Any group that is not composed of federal, state, tribal, county, city, town, local or other governmental entities.

objective: An objective is a concise target statement of what will be achieved, how much will be achieved, when and where it will be achieved, and who is responsible for the work. Objectives are derived from goals and provide the basis for determining management strategies. Objectives should be attainable and time-specific and should be stated quantitatively to the extent possible. If objectives cannot be stated quantitatively, they may be stated qualitatively (Draft Service Manual 602 FW 1.5).

plant community: An assemblage of plant species unique in its composition; occurs in particular locations under particular influences; a reflection or integration of the environmental influences on the site -- such as soil, temperature, elevation, solar radiation, slope, aspect, and rainfall; denotes a general kind of climax plant community, i.e., ponderosa pine or bunchgrass.

proposed action: The alternative proposed by the Service to best achieve the refuge purpose, vision, and goals; contributes to the Refuge System mission, addresses the significant issues; and is consistent with principles of sound fish and wildlife management.

priority public use: One of six uses authorized by the Improvement Act of 1997 to have priority if found to be compatible with a refuge's purposes. This includes hunting, fishing, wildlife observation, and photography, environmental education and interpretation.

public: Individuals, organizations, and groups; officials of federal, state, and local government agencies; Indian tribes; and foreign nations. It may include anyone outside the core planning team. It includes those who may or may not have indicated an interest in Service issues and those who do or do not realize that Service decisions may affect them.

public involvement: A process that offers affected and interested individuals and organizations an opportunity to learn about Service actions and policies and to express their opinions. The Service gives thoughtful consideration to public opinions when shaping decisions for refuge management.

purpose of the refuge: The purpose of a refuge is specified in, or derived from, the law, proclamation, executive order, agreement, public land order, donation document, or administrative memorandum establishing, authorization, or expanding a refuge,

refuge unit, or refuge subunit. (Draft Service Manual 602 FW 1.5).

refuge purpose: See purpose of the refuge.

refuge use: Any activity on a refuge, except for an administrative or law enforcement activity, carried out by, or under the direction of, an authorized Service employee.

restoration: Management emphasis designed to move ecosystems to desired conditions and processes, and/or to healthy upland habitats and aquatic systems.

riparian area or zone: An area or habitat that is transitional from a terrestrial to an aquatic ecosystem—includes streams, lakes wet areas, and adjacent plant communities and their associated soils which have free water at or near the surface; an area whose components are directly or indirectly attributed to the influence of water; of or relating to a river; specifically applied to ecology, "riparian" describes the land immediately adjoining and directly influenced by streams. For example, riparian vegetation includes any and all plant-life growing on the land adjoining a stream and directly influenced by the stream.

scoping: The process of obtaining information from the public for input into the planning process.

Service: See U.S. Fish and Wildlife Service.

shorebird: Any of a suborder (Charadrii) of birds (such as a plover or a snipe) that frequents the seashore or mud flat areas.

strategy: A specific action, tool, or technique—or combination of actions, tools, and techniques—used to meet unit objectives (Draft Service Manual 602 FW 1.5).

U.S. Fish and Wildlife Service (service, USFWS): The principal federal agency responsible for conserving, protecting, and enhancing fish and wildlife and their habitats for the continuing benefit of the American people. The Service manages the 93-million-acre Refuge System comprised of more than 530 refuges and thousands of waterfowl production areas. It also operates 65 national fish hatcheries and 78 ecological service field stations, the agency enforces federal wildlife laws, manages migratory bird populations, restores national significant fisheries, conserves and restores wildlife habitat such as wetlands, administers the Endangered Species Act, and helps foreign governments with their conservation efforts. It also oversees the Federal Aid program which distributes millions of dollars collected from excise taxes on fishing and hunting equipment to state wildlife agencies.

U.S. Fish and Wildlife Service mission: The mission of the U.S. Fish and Wildlife Service is working with others to conserve, protect, and enhance fish and wildlife and plants and their habitats for the continuing benefit of the American people.

USFWS: See U.S. Fish and Wildlife Service.

vision statement: A concise statement of the desired future condition of the planning unit, based primarily on the Refuge System mission, specific refuge purposes, and other relevant mandates (Draft Service Manual 602 FW 1.5).

warm-season grasses: Grasses that begin growth later in the season (early June). These grasses require warmer soil temperatures to germinate and actively grow when temperatures are warmer. Examples of warm season grasses are Indiangrass, switchgrass, and big bluestem.

waterfowl: A category of birds that includes ducks, geese, and swans.

watershed: The region draining into a river, river system, or body of water.

wildlife-dependent recreational use: The six priority public uses of the Refuge System as established in the Improvement Act are: hunting, fishing, wildlife observation and photography, and environmental education and interpretation." The Service also considers other wildlife-dependent uses in the preparation of CCPs; however, the six priority public uses always take precedence.

Appendices

Black-capped Chickadee
Tom Kelley/USFWS

Appendix A
Planning Team and Contributors

This plan is the result of the efforts by members of the planning team for Bear Butte NWR. The draft CCP and EA were written by refuge staff and the refuge planning team with input from other team members.

PLANNING TEAM

Name	Title	Agency
Linda Kelly	Planning Team Leader	USFWS
Tom Koerner	Project Leader	USFWS
Shilo Comeau	Refuge Biologist	USFWS

OTHER CONTRIBUTORS

Name	Title	Agency
Mimi Mather	Planner	Shapins and Associates
Tom Gibney	Planner	Shapins and Associates

NATIONAL WILDLIFE REFUGE MISSION, GOALS, AND GUIDING PRINCIPLES

The mission of the System is *"to administer a national network of lands and waters for the conservation, management, and where appropriate, restoration of the fish, wildlife, and plant resources and their habitats within the United States for the benefit of present and future generations of Americans"* (National Wildlife Refuge System Improvement Act of 1997).

GOALS OF THE NATIONAL WILDLIFE REFUGE SYSTEM ARE:

A. To fulfill our statutory duty to achieve refuge purpose(s) and further the System mission.

B. Conserve, restore where appropriate, and enhance all species of fish, wildlife, and plants that are endangered or threatened with becoming endangered.

C. Perpetuate migratory bird, inter-jurisdictional fish, and marine mammal populations.

D. Conserve a diversity of fish, wildlife, and plants.

E. Conserve and restore, where appropriate, representative ecosystems of the United States, including the ecological processes characteristic of those ecosystems.

F. To foster understanding and instill appreciation of fish, wildlife, and plants, and their conservation, by providing the public with safe, high-quality, and compatible wildlife-dependent public use. Such use includes hunting, fishing, wildlife observation and photography, and environmental education and interpretation.

There are four guiding principles for management and general public use of the refuge System established by Executive Order 12996 (3/25/96):

- **Public Use.** The Refuge System provides important opportunities for compatible wildlife-dependent recreational activities involving hunting, fishing, wildlife observation and photography, and environmental education and interpretation.

- **Habitat.** Fish and wildlife will not prosper without high quality habitat, and without fish and wildlife, traditional uses of refuge cannot be sustained. The Refuge System will continue to conserve and enhance the quality and diversity of fish and wildlife habitat within refuges.

- **Partnerships.** America's sportsmen and women were the first partners who insisted on protecting valuable wildlife habitat within wildlife refuges. Conservation partnerships with other Federal agencies, State agencies, Tribes, organizations, industry, and the general public can make significant contributions to the growth and management of the refuge System.

- **Public Involvement.** The public should be given a full and open opportunity to participate in decisions regarding acquisition and management of our national wildlife refuges.

LEGAL AND POLICY GUIDANCE

Management actions on national wildlife refuges are circumscribed by many mandates (laws, Executive Orders, etc.), the latest of which is the Volunteer and Community Partnership Enhancement Act of 1998. Regulations that affect refuge management the most are listed below.

National Wildlife Refuge System Improvement Act of 1997: Sets the mission and administrative policy for all refuges in the National Wildlife Refuge System; mandates comprehensive conservation planning for all units of the National Wildlife Refuge System.

Endangered Species Act (1973): Requires all Federal agencies to carry out programs for the conservation of endangered and threatened species.

National Environmental Policy Act (1969): Requires all agencies, including the Service, to examine the environmental impacts of their actions, incorporate environmental information, and use public participation in the planning and implementation of all actions. Federal agencies must integrate this Act with other planning requirements, and prepare appropriate documents to facilitate better environmental decision making (from 40 CFR 1500).

National Wildlife Refuge System Administration Act (1966): Defines the National Wildlife Refuge System and authorizes the Secretary to permit any use of a refuge, provided such use is compatible with the major purposes for which the refuge was established.

Refuge Recreation Act (1962): Allows the use of refuges for recreation when such uses are compatible with the refuge's primary purposes and when sufficient funds are available to manage the uses.

Fish and Wildlife Coordination Act (1958): Allows the Fish and Wildlife Service to enter into agreements with private landowners for wildlife management purposes.

Migratory Bird Conservation Act (1929): Establishes procedures for acquisition by purchase, rental, or gifts of areas approved by the Migratory Bird Conservation Commission.

Migratory Bird Treaty Act (1918): Designates the protection of migratory birds as a Federal responsibility. This Act enables the setting of seasons and other regulations, including the closing of areas, Federal or non-Federal, to the hunting of migratory birds.

Public scoping was completed in December 2004. A public meeting was held in Sturgis, South Dakota on December 2, 2004. Two people attended this meeting and in addition five written comments were received during the open-comment period. Comments received identified biological, social, and economic concerns regarding management.

MAILING LIST

The following mailing list was developed for this CCP.

FEDERAL OFFICIALS

U.S. Representative Stephanie Herseth, Washington DC; Rapid City, SD, Area Director

U.S. Senator Tim Johnson, Washington DC; Rapid City, SD, Area Director

U.S. Senator John Thune, Washington DC; Rapid City, SD, Area Director

FEDERAL AGENCIES LOCATED IN SOUTH DAKOTA

Bureau of Land Management, South Dakota Field Office, Belle Fourche

U.S. Fish and Wildlife Service Ecological Services, Pierre

Sand Lake National Wildlife Refuge and Wetland Management District

Huron Wetland Management District

Lake Andes National Wildlife Refuge and Wetland Management District

Karl Mundt National Wildlife Refuge

Madison Wetland Management District

Waubay Wildlife Refuge and Wetland Management District

USDA Forest Service, Black Hills National Forest, Custer

TRIBAL ORGANIZATIONS

Arapaho Business Council, Fort Washakie, WY

Black Feet Tribal Business Council, Browning, MT

Cheyenne River Sioux Tribe, Eagle Butte, SD

Chippewa Cree Business Committee, Box Elder, MT

Crow Creek Sioux Tribal Council, Fort Thompson, SD

Crow Tribal Council, Crow Agency, MT

Flandreau Santee Sioux Executive Committee, Flandreau, SD

Fort Belknap Community Council, Harlem, MT

Fort Peck Tribal Executive Board, Popular, MT

Lower Bruele Sioux Tribal Council, Lower Brule, SD

Northern Cheyenne Tribal Council, Lame Deer, MT

Oglala Sioux Tribal Council, Pine Ridge, SD

Omaha Tribal Council, Macy, NE

Ponca Tribe of Nebraska, Niobrara, NE

Rosebud Sioux Tribal Council, Rosebud, SD

Santee Sioux Tribal Council, Niobrara, NE

Shoshone Business Council, Fort Washakie, WY

Sisseton-Wahpeton Sioux Tribe, Agency Village, SD

Spirit Lake Tribal Council, Fort Totten, ND

Standing Rock Sioux Tribe, Fort Yates, ND

Three Affiliated Tribes, New Town, ND

Tribal Preservation Office, Standing Rock Sioux Tribe, Fort Yates, ND

Winnebago Tribal Council, Winnebago, NE

Yankton Sioux Tribe, Marty, SD

SOUTH DAKOTA STATE OFFICIALS

Senator Eric Bogue, Faith

Senator Kenneth McNenny, Sturgis

Senator J.P. Duniphan, Rapid City

Representative Thomas Brunner, Nisland

Representative Larry Rhoden, Union Center

Representative Michael Buckingham, Rapid City

Representative Don Can Etten, Rapid City

SOUTH DAKOTA STATE AGENCIES

Department of Agriculture, Pierre

Department of Emergency Management, Pierre

Department of Environment and Natural Resources, Pierre

Department of Game, Fish and Parks, Pierre and Lead

Division of Water Rights, Pierre

State Historic Preservation Officer, Pierre

State Conservationist, Pierre

Farm Bureau Federation, Huron

SOUTH DAKOTA LOCAL AGENCIES

City of Sturgis, South Dakota

Meade County Conservation District, Sturgis

Meade County Government, Sturgis

INDIVIDUALS

(10 people)

BIRDS

Loons & Grebes

Common Loon
Western Grebe
Horned Grebe
Eared Grebe
Pied-billed Grebe

Pelicans & Cormorants

American White Pelican
Double-crested Cormorant

Geese & Ducks

Canada Goose
Greater White-fronted Goose
Snow Goose
Mallard
Northern Pintail
Gadwall
American Wigeon
Northern Shoveler
Blue-winged Teal
Cinnamon Teal
Green-winged Teal
Wood Duck
Redhead
Canvasback
Ring-necked Duck
Lesser Scaup
Common Goldeneye
Bufflehead
Old Squaw
White-winged Scoter
Hooded Merganser
Red-breasted Merganser
Common Merganser
Ruddy Duck

Vultures, Hawks & Eagles

Turkey Vulture
Cooper's Hawk
Sharp-shinned Hawk

Northern Harrier
Rough-legged Hawk
Ferruginous Hawk
Red-tailed Hawk
Swainson's Hawk
Broad-winged Hawk
Bald Eagle
Golden Eagle
Osprey
Prairie Falcon
American Kestrel
Merlin

Gallinaceous Birds

Wild Turkey
Sharp-tailed Grouse
Ring-necked Pheasant
Gray Partridge

Herons

Great Blue Heron
Green-backed Heron
Yellow-crowned Night-heron

Cranes, Rails & Coots

Sandhill Crane
Sora Rail
American Coot

Shorebirds

American Avocet
Black-bellied Plover
Piping Plover
Killdeer
Marbled Godwit
Long-billed Curlew
Greater Yellowlegs
Lesser Yellowlegs
Solitary Sandpiper
Upland Sandpiper
Willet
Spotted Sandpiper
Short-billed Dowitcher

Long-billed Dowitcher
Wilson's Phalarope
Common Snipe
Least Sandpiper
Semi-palmated Sandpiper
Western Sandpiper

Gulls & Terns

Ring-billed Gull
Franklin Gull
Common Tern
Forster's Tern
Black Tern

Pigeons & Doves

Rock Dove
Mourning Dove

Cuckoos

Yellow-billed Cuckoo
Black-billed Cuckoo

Owls

Screech Owl
Great Horned Owl
Long-eared Owl
Short-eared Owl
Snow Owl
Northern Saw-whet

Goatsuckers, Swifts & Kingfishers

Common Nighthawk
Chimney Swift
Belted Kingfisher

Woodpeckers

Lewis' Woodpecker
Red-headed Woodpecker
Downy Woodpecker
Hairy Woodpecker
Northern Flicker

Flycatchers

Eastern Kingbird
Western Kingbird

Say's Phoebe
Least Flycatcher
Western Flycatcher
Trail's Flycatcher
Western Wood Pewee
Olive-sided Flycatcher

Larks

Horned Lark

Swallows

Barn Swallow
Cliff Swallow
Violet-green Swallow
Tree Swallow
Bank Swallow
Northern Rough-winged Swallow

Corvids

Blue Jay
Gray Jay
Black-billed Magpie
American Crow

Chickadees, Nuthatches & Creepers

Black-capped Chickadee
White-breasted Nuthatch
Red-breasted Nuthatch
Brown Creeper

Wrens

House Wren
Rock Wren
Canyon Wren
Marsh Wren

Thrashers & Thrushes

Gray Catbird
Brown Thrasher
American Robin
Townsend's Solitaire
Veery
Eastern Bluebird
Mountain Bluebird

Kinglets, Pipits & Waxwings

Ruby-crowned Kinglet
Water Pipit
Bohemian Waxwing
Cedar Waxwing

Shrikes & Starlings

Northern Shrike
Loggerhead Shrike
European Starling

Vireos & Warblers

Solitary Vireo
Red-eyed Vireo
Warbling Vireo
Black and White Warbler
Orange-crowned Warbler
Yellow Warbler
Yellow-rumped Warbler
  Myrtle race
  Audubon race
Ovenbird
Common Yellowthroat
Yellow-breasted Chat
American Redstart
Chestnut-sided Warbler
Blue-gray Gnatcatcher
Blue-winged Warbler

Weaver Finches

House Sparrow

Blackbirds & Orioles

Bobolink
Western Meadowlark
Yellow-headed Blackbird
Red-winged Blackbird

Brewer's Blackbird
Common Grackle
Brown-headed Cowbird
Orchard Oriole
Northern Oriole

Tanagers, Grosbeaks & Others

Western Tanager
Rose-breasted Grosbeak
Black-headed Grosbeak
Evening Grosbeak
Blue Grosbeak
Indigo Bunting
Lazuli Bunting
Rosy Finch
Common Redpoll
Pine Siskin
American Goldfinch
Red Crossbill
Rufous-sided Towhee

Sparrows & Longspurs

Savannah Sparrow
Grasshopper Sparrow
Lark Bunting
Vesper Sparrow
Lark Sparrow
Junco, Dark-eyed
  Slate-colored race
  White-winged race
  Oregon race
American Tree Sparrow
Chipping Sparrow
Clay-colored Sparrow
Field Sparrow
Harris' Sparrow
White-crowned Sparrow
White-throated Sparrow
Song Sparrow
Chestnut-collared Longspur

DIVESTITURE MODEL DISCUSSION

The planning team ran the divestiture model to determine whether Bear Butte National Wildlife Refuge should be considered for divestiture. The results are below.

Date: March 30, 2005
Place: Lacreek National Wildlife Refuge

Attendance

Service personnel and Shapins Associates

Summary

Although the refuge has supported migratory bird and fish populations, the level of support has not been substantial. The State's recreational goals have conflicted with Refuge System goals. Restoration of the refuge's biological integrity would necessitate removal of state park facilities. The Service has not maintained the refuge since 1967 and, therefore, its rights to the land would probably not be upheld in court.

PRIMARY CONSIDERATIONS

1. Does the refuge achieve one or more of the Refuge System goals?

Yes. The refuge achieves some of the Refuge System goals by providing a resting and watering spot for migrating birds, supporting native plants, and by fostering an understanding and instilling appreciation of fish, wildlife, and plants, and their conservation.

2. Does it contribute to landscape conservation, provide a stepping stone for migratory birds or serve as a unique habitat patch important to the conservation of a trust species?

Partially. The refuge contains a body of water in an arid part of the State. Therefore, it is somewhat of a "stepping stone for migratory birds." The rest of the statement does not apply with regard to this refuge.

3. Does the refuge provide substantial support for migratory bird species, provide important sheltering, feeding and breeding habitat for threatened and endangered species, or support species identified in authorizing legislation?

No. The support the refuge provides does not meet the definition of "substantial." One-day estimates at Bear Butte Lake rarely exceed 200 birds. By comparison one day estimates at Lacreek National Wildlife Refuge have documented 60,000 birds. The refuge does not substantially contribute to the survival of threatened or endangered plant or animal species.

4. Does the refuge fulfill its mission as stated in the Improvement Act?

No. The refuge has probably never fulfilled its mission because its purpose was to provide a recreational area for the surrounding communities. Because of this public-use disturbance, the refuge is not an inviolate sanctuary. The conflicting purposes of the Service and the State have been discussed as far back as the 1950s. The Service's answer to this dilemma was to allow the State to maintain the refuge under the cooperative agreement of 1967.

5. Does the refuge have biological integrity; if not, is it feasible to restore the biological integrity of the converted or degraded habitat?

No. Bear Butte Lake is a natural wetland increased in size with a dam and diverted flows and it is not feasible to remove it. The habitat is not "degraded" but the recreational uses do not allow for the land to be an inviolate habitat for plant and animal species.

6. Does the Service have, or can it reasonably acquire, the right to restore the habitat?

No. The Service has not enforced the rights contained in the easement for many years; neither has it made its rights known. For these reasons, the Service's rights to the land would probably not stand up in court.

Bibliography

Green, J.; and Short, N.M. 1971. Volcanic landforms and surface features: a photographic atlas and glossary. NY: Springer Verlag. 519 p.

Karner, F.R.; and Halvorson, D.L. 1987. The Devils Tower, Bear Lodge Mountains: cenozoic igneous complex. In Beus, S.S., ed., Centennial Field Guide. Volume 2. Geological Society of America, Rocky Mountain Section. p. 161–164.

Bureau of Land Management and South Dakota Game, Fish and Parks Department. 1991. Birds of the Fort Meade Recreation Area and Bear Butte State Park. Bear Butte State Park, SD.

Chief, division of realty, region 6, U.S. Fish and Wildlife Service. Memo dated May 26, 2004. U.S. Fish and Wildlife Service.

South Dakota Game, Fish and Parks Department. 2003. South Dakota Statewide Fisheries Survey 2102-F21-R-36. Pierre, SD.

U.S. Census Bureau Quick Facts. 2002.

U.S. Fish and Wildlife Service. 2005. Draft comprehensive conservation plan and environmental assessment, Kirwin National Wildlife Refuge. Denver, CO.

U.S. Fish and Wildlife Service. 2002. Birds of conservation concern. U.S. Fish and Wildlife Service, division of migratory bird management. Arlington, VA. <http://migratorybirds.fws.gov/reports/BCC2002.pdf.>

Encyclopedia entry for the Black Hills of South Dakota: <http://www.en.wikipedia.org/wiki/Black_Hills> 1/15/05

Encyclopedia entry for Sturgis, South Dakota: <http://www.en.wikipedia.org/wiki/Sturgis_South_Dakota> 11/16/05

National Oceanic and Atmospheric Administration entry for the climate of South Dakota: <http://www.noaa.gov/climate/southdakota> 11/16/05

National Park Service entry for Wind Cave National Park: <http://www.nps.gov/wica/Grasses_of_the_Mixed_Grass_Prairie.htm> 2/15/06

State park entry for Bear Butte State Park in South Dakota: <http://www/sdgfp.info/parks/regions/westriver/bearbutte2.htm> 11/15/05

State website entry for the air quality statistics in South Dakota: <http://www.state.sd.us/denr/DES/air quality/airprog>